PREFACE

Dear Children,

This special little book is like an email—or a postcard, if you know what that is—from when your parents—or, perhaps your grandparents —were children. Maybe they cooked the recipes from these pages—I certainly did! Each drawing and every delicious description made me want to prepare every recipe! Opening the book cover and finding the treats within—and especially the possibility of making them on my own —was the most wonderful thing. It still is!

Of course, the world is a different place now from when your parents and grandparents were little. Some of the foods we eat are the same, but some may be very different. For example, your family might keep kosher, or might not; maybe you or your family are vegetarians, vegans, or locavores; we may eat spicy food often, and foods from all over the world, or we may eat much plainer food; our food at home is whatever way our families choose to eat, and are able to eat (sometimes there are foods that we simply can't eat, for example, children who are allergic to gluten, to nuts, or to dairy products). We have many more possibilities and choices than your parents and grandparents did.

For instance, in this book, there are a number of recipes for cottage cheese; in "the old days," cottage cheese was a mainstay of the daily diet. Nowadays you might be used to eating all kinds of cheeses: there are also other milky soft cheeses that are eaten in addition to or in place of cottage cheese, such as ricotta, mild goat cheese, or Greek yogurt. So, when preparing the dishes from this book, we can use these other cheeses instead of cottage cheese (at least sometimes).

And not just cottage cheese. In the past, milk was always cow (sometimes goat) milk, usually either whole or skim; nowadays we have not only different types of cow milk, we also have "milks" made from nuts, grains, and seeds such as almond milk, soy milk and oat milk. In the 1950s and 1960s, most families didn't know about avocados, artichokes, and olives, while now many of us eat them often—their goodness has spread throughout the world's tables.

And who knew hummus then? Today almost anywhere you go in the world everyone knows what hummus is, so it's fun to see the differences between then and now. You and your parents/grandparents can cook together and talk about the differences between their childhood holiday foods and yours.

All over the world, today, Jewish communities are in touch with one another—in your parents' and grandparents' time this was not so. For example, maybe your older brother or sister visited Israel as part of Taglit, which brings young Jewish people to visit and learn about Israel, including new things to eat and cook! We are so lucky that we are able to get to know each other's cultures and ways to celebrate—especially with food! And we are influencing each other through tasting each other's foods!

When your grandparents, even your parents, were young, most of the "Jewish" food was very different from now; for one thing, it was more Ashkenazi (Eastern European). Ashkenazi food usually didn't have a lot of spices—maybe salt and pepper—and probably lots of onions and garlic. Some Ashkenazi Jews (especially those from Poland) liked their foods quite sweet.

We called our grandparents Bubbe and Zayde—many spoke Yiddish—and ate tzimmes, blintzes, and kugel, and oh, at the Bar and Bat Mitzvot, how the aunties, grandmas and mothers would make Mandelbrot, jam-filled cookies, and as many traditional sweet things as they could!

Now, we are Jewish in many different ways; we could be Orthodox, Conservative, Reconstructionist, Reform, observant, or not very religious at all. Your family could be Israeli, Ashkenazi, Sephardic, or Iranian, Italian, Ethiopian, or even Chinese, or mixed of different origins, some Jewish, some not. We come from everywhere. And today, in addition to the women in your family, it might be your father, grandfather, or uncle making the cookies, or cakes, or chicken matzo ball soup. You may be used to eating such foods as chia seeds, avocado, whole grains, edamame, almond milk, sriracha, tofu, veggie-burgers, and so forth, even in your Jewish festival treats.

This book gives you a taste of what it was like being a Jewish child in America in the 1950s and 1960s. As Aunt Fanny writes in the introduction of this book, these are the "foods you like to eat!" Your grandparents and parents liked to eat them then, and many are what you like to eat now. Matzo brei, for example, and buttered noodles with cottage cheese (savory or sweet). And while you may have different fruits and spices in your charoset, the recipe in this little book for Ashkenazi apple and walnut charoset is JUST THE WAY we made it at home when I was a tiny child, and the way I make it now. It is super-delicious. And you can make it too!

And, as a little addition to Aunt Fanny's book, we're adding a special collection just for you of right-now recipes, and the holidays to which they belong.

A few things have changed in the world of cooking since Aunt Fanny wrote this book, so I thought I'd point some out to you.

Double Boiler Any recipe that calls for using a double boiler, especially for chocolate, can be easily done in the microwave:

1. Use a microwave-safe dish and set the microwave to High/Cook for 45 seconds.

2. Take the bowl out, stir it up, and then put it back in for another 45 seconds.

3. Take it out again and stir it; the chocolate should have melted completely, but if it hasn't, microwave it one more time.

You can also use the microwave for steaming prunes and other fruit: using a microwave-safe dish, stew the fruit on High for 45 seconds.

Potato Kugel A potato kugel is a big flat casserole of potato, which looks kind of like a big baked—instead of fried—latke.

Penuche One of the recipes is for Penuche, which is an old-fashioned word for brown sugar fudge.

Canned Fruit A lot of recipes that use canned fruit can now be made with fresh fruit if it's in season, for example, pears.

I also added a few comments in the footnotes of the book where some of the information about holidays and dates has gotten a bit confusing. I think Aunt Fanny would have appreciated that!

YaYa (Grandma) Marlena Spieler

VERY IMPORTANT TO READ!

Before you start cooking these wonderful dishes, and while you're very grown up already, there are some things you must have a grownup around to help you with:

• Cutting anything with a sharp knife!

• Using the oven or stovetop, especially double boilers and fry pans!

• Using the microwave—making sure you put in microwave-safe dishes and setting the microwave correctly!

• Any frying—deep or even just in butter—can splatter and cause really painful burns, so always, always have a grownup on hand!

During Aunt Fanny's time, children were allowed to do a lot of things we don't allow today (like ride bikes without helmets!), so this is why you must follow these safety instructions when cooking today!

Dear Junior Cook:

This Junior Jewish Cook Book is written especially for you. The recipes are simple, and each step is outlined clearly, so that you will easily be able to follow all the directions.

The recipes are for foods you like to eat, and we hope you enjoy making the recipes as well as eating them.

Notice too, that the Cook Book is divided into holiday sections. Every section contains a short story of the holiday and its customs and ceremonies, and every recipe has been placed in its very own holiday section.

You will learn to make different kinds of holiday delicacies, so you'll be able to prepare menus for your very own parties!

You'll have a wonderful surprise for Mother too, because you are going to keep your kitchen neat and clean; Mother will never guess that you've been working there.

We hope you have lots of fun cooking!

Aunt Fanny

**All the recipes in this book are in accordance
with the Jewish dietary laws.**

CONTENTS

APPENDIX:
MODERN JEWISH RECIPES

EQUIPMENT

ICE TRAY

CASSEROLE

STRAINER

WOODEN FORK

DOUBLE BOILER

WOODEN SPOON

APPLE CORER

WOODEN BOWL

GRATER

PARING KNIFE

PANCAKE TURNER

COLANDER

SAUCEPANS

MUFFIN PAN

CLOCK

SPATULA

SCISSORS

COOKIE SHEET

POTS

EGG BEATER

POT HOLDERS

MEASURING CUPS

PAPER TOWEL

LONG FORK

BUTTER KNIFE

COOLING RACK

BAKING PAN

TONGS

SHALLOW PAN

LONG SPOON

TABLE FORK

FRUIT JUICER

MIXING BOWLS

MEASURING SPOONS

VEGETABLE BRUSH

FLOUR SIFTER

CHOPPING KNIFE

KITCHEN TABLESPOON

BREAD BOARD

FRYING PAN

SLICING KNIFE

EQUIVALENTS

 **3 TEASPOONS**
equal
1 TABLESPOON

 **4 TABLESPOONS**
equal
¼ CUP

 **2 CUPS**
equal
1 PINT

 **¼ POUND BUTTER**
equals
½ CUP

BEFORE COOKING RULES

1. Wear a clean apron.
2. Scrub your hands well.
3. Open the book to the recipe you are using and keep the pages down with rubber bands.
4. Assemble all your ingredients and equipment.

AFTER COOKING RULES

1. Always leave the kitchen as clean as it was when you started cooking.
2. Put away all ingredients in the same places from which they came.
3. Wash all utensils you have used, dry them and put them away in the correct place.
4. Clean and dry the work table.
5. Sweep the floor and wipe up any liquids you may have spilled.
6. Wash the sink.
7. Hang up your apron and the towels you have used.

MEASURING SUGGESTIONS

1. Always be sure to use the exact amounts given in the recipe.
2. Always pour liquids to the exact top of the glass, cup, or spoon.
3. Have a set of measuring cups and spoons.
4. Always measure dry ingredients first.
5. Next measure liquids.
6. Next measure fats.
7. Before starting to cook, light the oven and bring it to the proper temperature.

SAFETY RULES

1. Always ask an adult's permission before using the kitchen.
2. Always ask a grownup to light the stove for you.
3. Use a pot holder to lift hot dishes.
4. Turn the pot handles towards the back of the stove.
5. Use wooden spoons for stirring hot foods, because wood does not conduct heat.
6. Always have your work table clean.

COOKING TERMS

BASTE To pour liquid or fat over food which is cooking to moisten or flavor it.

DICE To cut to tiny pieces.

BEAT To mix by hand, by beater, or by electric mixer.

BAKE To cook in an oven by dry heat.

BLEND To mix shortening into dry ingredients.

BROIL To cook under direct fire.

CREAM To mix shortening until smooth, soft and creamy.

FRY To cook in hot fat or in deep oil.

ROAST To cook uncovered in the oven with moisture.

GRATE To rub food on a grater.

BOIL To cook in a liquid which has been brought to a boil and left there.

RULES OF ETIQUETTE

1. Always wash your hands before starting to eat.
2. Sit straight up on the chair, never slouch or lean.
3. Take only as much food as you know you can eat.
4. Eat quietly without making any undue noise.
5. Take only small bits of food and eat slowly.
6. Never reach across the table.
   Ask to have the food passed to you.
7. Don't be afraid to try a new food. All food is good.
8. Always say a prayer before and after eating.

   Thank you God,
   For bread and meat,
   We pray that others too,
   May have enough to eat.

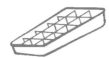

HOW TO SET YOUR TABLE

PUT YOUR MILK OR WATER GLASS HERE

PUT YOUR NAPKIN HERE — FOLDED

HERE'S WHERE YOUR SILVERWARE GOES

AND HERE'S HOW YOUR TABLE SHOULD LOOK ALL READY TO SIT DOWN

SHABBAT

In every Jewish home, Friday is a busy day. Before sundown, the house is thoroughly cleaned, and the Shabbat table set.

How nice the Shabbat table looks with the beautiful white tablecloth, gleaming candlesticks, shiny silver wine cups, and golden twisted challahs.

The Shabbat starts when Mother lights the candles. The children watch in fascination as she covers her eyes with her hands and in the glowing candlelight recites the blessing.

Soon afterwards, Father or Mother pours the ruby-red wine into a silver wine cup, raises it, and sings the Kiddush. Then, the Ha-Motzi is said over the challah, and a slice of it is given to everyone at the table.

Now, the supper is served: chicken soup, clear and golden, roast chicken, gefilte fish, and scrumptious kugel. What a feast!

After supper, as soon as the dishes are cleared away, the family sings Shabbat songs.

The next morning everyone is up bright and early, and off to temple they go. The youngsters hold their own service. Some of them act as cantors; some of them read the Torah; all of them join in singing the Shabbat prayers just as the grownups do.

The Shabbat ends when the first three stars appear in the sky. Then it is time for the Havdalah ceremony. A blessing is recited over a cup of wine, a besamin box filled with spices, and a twisted Havdalah candle.

The Havdalah ceremony is really a way of saying "goodbye" to the Shabbat until next Friday night.

SHABBAT CANDLESTICK SALAD

INGREDIENTS
canned sliced pineapple
lettuce
bananas
cherries

EQUIPMENT
knife
plate
can opener

HOW TO MAKE
1. Wash a lettuce leaf and shake off the water.
2. Dry it on a plate.
3. Place a slice of pineapple on the lettuce leaf.
   This is the base for the candlestick.
4. Cut a banana half crosswise and stand it in the pineapple hole.
   This is the candle.
5. Place a cherry on top of the banana. This is the candle flame.

SHABBAT DELIGHTS

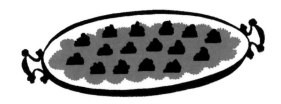

No Shabbat is complete without cookies.
Here's an easy recipe that's a "delight" to taste.

INGREDIENTS

6 oz package semi-sweet chocolate pieces
½ cup graham cracker crumbs
1 cup broken walnuts

EQUIPMENT

measuring cup
wax paper
wooden spoon
double boiler

HOW TO MAKE

1. Melt chocolate in a double boiler.
2. Stir in graham cracker crumbs and walnuts.
3. Drop mixture from teaspoon onto wax paper.
4. Let stand until cool.
5. Makes about 15 delights.

FRIED FISH

Fish has always played an important part in all holiday and Shabbat meals. Serve cold fried fish at your Saturday and holiday afternoon meals. Serve fish with potato salad and pickles.

INGREDIENTS

1 pound fish fillets, haddock, halibut or flounder
1 teaspoon salt
a pinch of pepper
¼ cup matzoh meal
1 tablespoon water
frying oil
1 egg

EQUIPMENT

knife
fry pan
shallow plate
fork
paper toweling
bowl
measuring cup
egg beater

HOW TO MAKE

1. Beat 1 egg.
2. Add water to beaten egg and beat slightly.
3. Mix the pepper and salt with the matzoh meal.
4. Dip the fish slices in the beaten egg and then in the matzoh mixture.
5. Pour oil in fry pan until ⅛ inch deep.
6. Heat up the frying oil.
7. Carefully place the dipped fish slices in the hot oil (make sure there is a grownup around to help you with this!)
8. Brown first one side and then the other.
9. Place fish on paper toweling and drain excess fat.
10. Serve hot or cold.

BOILED NOODLES

No Friday night meal is complete without Goldene Yuch, "golden" chicken soup. Noodles make a fine garnish for this Shabbat delicacy.

INGREDIENTS

¼ pound noodles
2 teaspoons salt
2 quarts boiling water

EQUIPMENT

large pot
colander

HOW TO MAKE

1. Break noodles into pieces about 2 inches long.
2. Add salt to boiling water.
3. Add noodles gradually.
4. Cook the noodles for about 10 minutes, stirring constantly.
5. Drain in colander.
6. Rinse with boiling water.
7. Add noodles to soup.
8. Or, add 3 teaspoons melted butter and serve as a vegetable.

CANDIED SWEET POTATOES

Candied sweet potatoes will make a welcome addition to any Shabbat meal.

INGREDIENTS

4 sweet potatoes
½ cup brown sugar
¼ cup melted butter
¼ cup water

EQUIPMENT

large pot
scrubbing brush
saucepan
knife

HOW TO MAKE

1. Scrub the sweet potatoes well.
2. Cook the potatoes well for 35 minutes with their skins on.
3. Peel the jackets from the potatoes.
4. Slice each potato into quarters lengthwise.
5. Place sliced hot potatoes into saucepan.
6. Mix the sugar, butter and water together.
7. Add the mixture to the potatoes.
8. Simmer over low heat, turning frequently, till all the potatoes are glazed.

POTATO KUGEL

Kugel is one of those dishes that is everyone's favorite.

INGREDIENTS

5 big potatoes
½ cup matzoh meal
3 eggs
salt and pepper
oil, shortening or butter

EQUIPMENT

grater
measuring cup
beater
baking dish or fry pan

HOW TO MAKE

1. Grate potatoes.
2. Add matzoh meal, salt, and pepper.
3. Separate the eggs into yolks and egg whites.
4. Add well-beaten egg yolks.
5. Beat egg whites stiff and fold into mixture.
6. Pour into greased baking dish.
7. Bake until brown on top.

ROSH HASHANA

The first ten days of the Jewish New Year are called the High Holy Days. The High Holy Days start with the holiday of Rosh Hashana, which means New Year.

On Rosh Hashana we go to temple. There we pray that God will send us blessings in the coming year, and we thank God for the blessings we have experienced in the year which passed.

At the end of the service, it is customary for everyone to turn to his or her neighbor and say a "Happy New Year."

At home, Rosh Hashana begins with the lighting of the candles and the singing of Kiddush.

On the table stands a round challah and a bowl of apple slices and honey. The round challah signifies a year without end. The apple slices and honey symbolize our hope for a "sweet and happy New Year."

YOM KIPPUR

The last day of the High Holy Days is called Yom Kippur (day of atonement). This holiday is the holiest day of the year and is devoted to fasting and prayer.

The Yom Kippur eve service begins with the beautiful Kol Nidre prayer; and the fasting is continuous for twenty-four hours.

On Yom Kippur eve, it is advisable to serve no spiced food. The meal at the end of the fast can be composed of regular Shabbat dishes.

HONEY CARROT TZIMMES

The Jewish (or Yiddish) word for carrot is "merin" which also means "to increase." During the High Holy Days carrots are served in various forms. They symbolize our hope for a year of "increasing" health and "increasing" prosperity.

INGREDIENTS

1 pound carrots
¼ teaspoon salt
¼ cup honey
1 tablespoon flour
dash of lemon juice
3 tablespoons butter

EQUIPMENT

deep pot
knife
peeler
fry pan
measuring cup
measuring spoon

HOW TO MAKE

1. Peel carrots and cut into thin slices.
2. Cover carrots with cold water and cook for 10 minutes.
3. Add the salt, honey, and lemon juice.
4. Let boil gently for about 15 minutes; until liquid has been reduced to about half.
5. Brown flour in hot melted butter.
6. Add to carrot mixture and shake gently.
7. Cook for 5 minutes more.

ROSH HASHANA CLUSTERS

Start the New Year right. Here's a "treat" that will make the New Year "sweet."

INGREDIENTS

1 cup semi-sweet chocolate bits
8 marshmallows cut into small pieces
¼ cup seedless raisins
¾ cup chopped walnuts

EQUIPMENT

double boiler
measuring cup
teaspoon
wax paper
wooden spoon

HOW TO MAKE

1. Melt chocolate over double boiler.
2. Mix in marshmallows, raisins, and walnuts.
3. Stir till all ingredients are coated.
4. Drop by teaspoon on wax paper.
5. Let stand and cool.
6. Makes about 18 clusters.

STUFFED EGGS

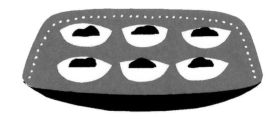

To the Jews the egg has always been a symbol of life. It is appropriate to serve egg dishes during the High Holy Days in the hope that the coming New Year will be filled with life and happiness.

INGREDIENTS

3 hard–boiled eggs
2 tablespoons mayonnaise
¼ teaspoon salt
speck pepper
1 teaspoon diced onion
⅛ teaspoon mustard

EQUIPMENT

knife
fork
wax paper
measuring spoon

HOW TO MAKE

1. Shell the eggs, cut in half lengthwise and lay whites aside.
2. Carefully remove yolks and mash.
3. Mix the yolks with the salt, mayonnaise, pepper, mustard and diced onion.
4. Refill the egg whites.

HONEY COOKIES

Honey is symbolic of the wish for a "sweet and happy New Year." Serve these cookies and start the New Year right.

INGREDIENTS

1 cup butter
½ cup sugar
4 tablespoons honey
2½ cups sifted all-purpose flour

EQUIPMENT

spoon
wax paper
rolling pin
cookie cutters
baking sheet
measuring cup
measuring spoon
fork

HOW TO MAKE

1. Cream butter, sugar and honey.
2. Add flour slowly.
3. Mix thoroughly to a smooth dough.
4. Chill in refrigerator for 2 hours.
5. Roll out on wax paper to about ½ inch thick.
6. Shape with a cookie cutter.
7. Place on ungreased cookie sheet.
8. Bake in oven at 300 degrees for 25 minutes.

BAKED POTATO

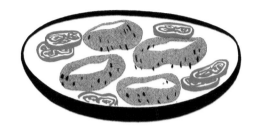

A baked potato is a welcome addition to any meal.

INGREDIENTS
potatoes
salt

EQUIPMENT
oven rack

HOW TO MAKE
1. Preheat oven to 400 degrees.
2. Wash the potatoes well.
3. Sprinkle well with salt.
4. Bake on rack for 1 hour.

SUKKOT

Sukkot (Feast of Booths) is celebrated for eight days. On this occasion we recall the booths in which the Hebrews lived during their wanderings from Egypt to the Promised Land.

On this holiday, we too build Sukkot (booths) and roof them with boughs and vines of green, just as our ancestors did thousands of years ago.

Sukkot is also known as the Harvest Festival. In honor of the festival we decorate the inside of the Sukkah booth with fruit and flowers.

As symbols of the ancient harvest in the land of Israel, we recite blessings over the Lulav (palm), the Etrog (citron), the Hadas (Myrtus), and the Arava (willow).

Since Sukkot is the Harvest Festival, it is customary to eat fruits, vegetables, and dairy dishes.

SIMCHAT TORAH

The last day of Sukkot is known as Simchat Torah (Rejoicing of the Law). On this day we read the last chapter of the Torah and we start our Torah all over again by also reading the first chapter.

After the reading, all the Torah scrolls are taken from the Ark and the Hakafot (procession) begins. The holy scrolls are carried around the temple seven times. Even those who are not carrying Torah scrolls join in the parade. They march behind the Torah carrying flags and singing happy Simchat Torah songs. Before the Hakafot the children are given bags of candy and nuts and a juicy red apple.

With Simchat Torah, the holiday of Sukkot comes to a happy end.

SIMCHAT TORAH
FLAG SALAD

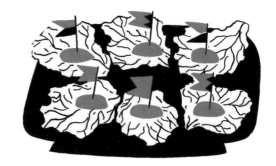

INGREDIENTS
  canned peaches
  lettuce

EQUIPMENT
  knife
  plate
  toothpicks
  paper
  can opener
  scissors

HOW TO MAKE
1. Wash a lettuce leaf, shake off the water and lay it on the plate.
2. Place half a peach on the lettuce leaf, flat side up.
3. Cut out a piece of paper into a flag and put it on a toothpick.
4. Stick the toothpick into the peach.
5. You can color the flag or write the name of a guest on the flag.

PENUCHE

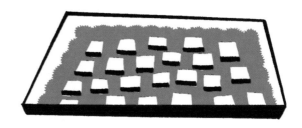

INGREDIENTS

2 cups brown sugar
⅔ cup milk
4 tablespoons butter
1 cup nuts or raisins
½ teaspoon vanilla
butter, oil, or shortening

EQUIPMENT

measuring cup
measuring spoon
wooden spoon
saucepan
beater

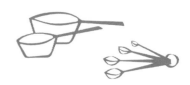

HOW TO MAKE

1. Mix sugar, milk and butter in saucepan.
2. Bring to boil.
3. Cook slowly for 15 minutes.
4. Remove from fire.
5. Add nuts and vanilla and beat till creamy.
6. Pour into shallow greased pan to cool.
7. When cool, cut into squares.

CARROT RAISIN SALAD

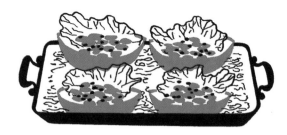

Serve this salad at your Sukkot party.

INGREDIENTS

2 carrots
½ cup raisins
mayonnaise
lettuce

EQUIPMENT

scrubbing brush
cutting board
knife
bowl
measuring cup
spoon

HOW TO MAKE

1. Wash a lettuce leaf and shake off the water.
2. Lay it on a plate.
3. Wash the carrots and dice.
4. Dice the raisins.
5. Place raisins and carrots in bowl.
6. Mix in mayonnaise.
7. Place a scoop of salad on a lettuce leaf.
8. Makes 4 portions.

BAKED BANANAS

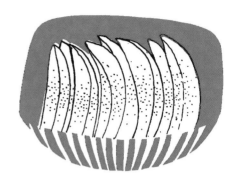

Fruit dishes and fruit desserts are traditional for Sukkot.
Try this simple recipe on your family.
They'll want you to make it often.

INGREDIENTS

6 hard bananas
2 tablespoons butter
2 tablespoons brown sugar

EQUIPMENT

baking pan

HOW TO MAKE

1. Peel green firm bananas and place in greased baking pan.
2. Brush with butter.
3. Sprinkle with brown sugar.
4. Bake at 375 degrees for 18 minutes.
5. Serve as a hot vegetable.
6. Or, as a dessert with cream.

MEATBURGERS

Meatburgers are everyone's favorite.
Try these as a main dish for one of your Sukkot meals.

INGREDIENTS

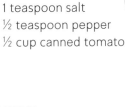

1 pound ground meat
¼ cup bread crumbs
1 egg
1 teaspoon salt
½ teaspoon pepper
½ cup canned tomatoes

EQUIPMENT

fork
baking pan
knife
measuring cup
measuring spoon

HOW TO MAKE

1. Dice canned tomatoes
2. Mix ground meat with bread crumbs, egg, salt, pepper and diced canned tomatoes.
3. Shape into patties 1 inch thick.
4. Bake in hot oven at 450 degrees for 12 minutes.

THE STORY OF CHANUKAH

Many years ago, a wicked Syrian[1] king named Antiochus captured the land of Israel. He ordered the Jews to give up their religion and worship his idols. All who refused to obey the king's command were put to death.

Under the leadership of Mattityahu and his five sons, the Jews rebelled. Even though they were greatly outnumbered by the Syrian forces, the courageous Maccabean army defeated the enemy and captured Jerusalem.

Immediately, they marched to the Holy Temple and smashed the idols that the Syrians had put there. When they cleaned and repaired the Temple, everyone gathered to celebrate the "rededication."

The high priest could find only one flask of Holy Oil with which to light the new menorah. This was just enough oil to burn for one day. But a great miracle happened! Much to everyone's amazement, this little flask of oil burnt for eight days and nights. Because of this miracle we celebrate Chanukah for eight days.

Chanukah comes on the 25th day of Kislev, in the deep of the winter. On the first night of Chanukah we light one candle, and every night thereafter we light an additional one until our menorah has eight candles standing in a row.

When the menorah is lit, and the blessings are sung, the festivities begin. Everyone gathers around the menorah and joins in playing draydel games and exchanging Chanukah gifts.

The traditional food for Chanukah is "latkes" (potato pancakes). The reason for eating this food is uncertain.[2]

---

1. Actually, Antiochus was a Hellenistic king who came from the area today known as Syria. Easy to get confused, I know.

2. You probably already know that the traditional food for Chanukah is food cooked in oil to symbolize the miracle of the *menorah*. In Israel they eat *sufganiot*, in Middle Eastern countries they eat fried pastries, and in the United States, we eat latkes.

Some say we eat latkes because the Maccabees used to eat them. When chasing their enemies, they did not have time to stop and eat a regular meal, so they ate latkes, which are easy and quick to prepare.

CHANUKAH COOKIES

If you do not have any cookie cutters, here are some patterns for you to trace. Make them out of cardboard and cut around them.

INGREDIENTS

2 cups flour
1 cup sugar
½ teaspoon salt
2 teaspoons baking powder
1 egg
⅓ cup butter
¼ cup milk
1 teaspoon vanilla
butter, oil, or shortening

EQUIPMENT

large bowl
measuring cup
measuring spoon
beater
sifter
bread board
rolling pin
cookie cutters
cookie sheet

HOW TO MAKE

1. Cream butter and sugar in a large bowl.
2. In another bowl, beat the egg and add the milk and flavoring.
3. Stir both mixes into a large bowl.
4. Sift together the flour, salt, and baking powder.
5. Add these ingredients into the large mixture and stir well.
6. Place the dough into the refrigerator for one hour.
7. Dust a bread board and rolling pin with flour.
8. Roll out the cool dough about ¼ inch thick.
9. Cut into fancy shapes with cookie cutters.
10. Place on a greased cookie sheet.
11. Bake in oven for 12 minutes.

CHANUKAH LATKES

Latkes, latkes, yum, yum, yum
Try this recipe and you'll make some
Latkes, latkes, they'll taste fine,
I'll bet you'll make them all the time.

INGREDIENTS

2 large potatoes
½ an onion
1 egg
¼ cup flour
1 teaspoon salt
oil, butter, or shortening

EQUIPMENT

grater
mixing bowl
beater
fry pan
spoon
paper toweling
spatula
measuring cup
paring knife

HOW TO MAKE

1. Peel the potatoes and grate.
2. Peel and grate the onion.
3. Add the flour, salt and egg.
4. Mix thoroughly till smooth.
5. Grease the fry pan.
6. Drop the batter into the hot fry pan, making each pancake about three inches in diameter.
7. Fry till brown on one side; then turn to other side and also fry till brown.
8. Lift from fry pan and place on paper toweling till fat drains off.

MARSHMALLOW POPS

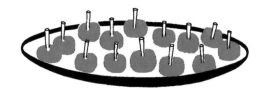

These marshmallow pops will really make a hit at your Chanukah party.

INGREDIENTS

marshmallow
water
chopped pecans

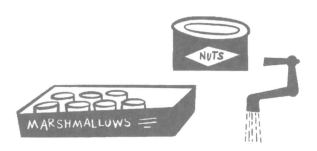

EQUIPMENT

saucepan
wax paper
short drinking straws (or popsicle sticks)
long fork

HOW TO MAKE

1. Stick marshmallow onto a long kitchen fork.
2. Steam over boiling water until sticky.
3. Drop marshmallow on chopped pecan and roll until coated.
4. Place on wax paper till coated marshmallow is firm.
5. Stick straws/sticks into each.

DRAYDEL SALAD

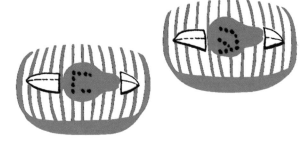

Here is an easy Chanukah surprise to make.

INGREDIENTS
- canned pear halves
- raisins
- banana

EQUIPMENT
- knife
- can opener

HOW TO MAKE
1. Place pear half on plate, flat side down.
2. Use raisins to make a draydel letter.
3. Cut bananas into long slices.
4. Use one slice for the handle of the draydel.
5. Use a short slice for the tip of the draydel.

PANCAKES

INGREDIENTS

    1 cup pancake mix
    shortening, oil, or butter
    maple syrup

EQUIPMENT

    griddle
    spatula
    spoon
    large bowl
    paper toweling
    measuring cup

HOW TO MAKE

1. Prepare the pancake mix according to the directions on the box.
2. Stir well and leave no lumps.
3. Heat the griddle and grease with shortening, keep the heat on medium.
4. Spoon pancake mixture into hot griddle; each pancake should be about 4 inches in diameter.
5. When edges look brown and the bubbles start to break, turn the pancake with your spatula.
6. Cook till brown on the other side.
7. Remove from griddle and serve with butter and syrup.

CHAMISHAH ASAR B'SHEVAT

A rbor Day in Israel is called Chamishah Asar B'Shevat[1] (which means "the fif-teenth day of the month of Shevat"). It is a very big and important holiday there.

On this day, all the synagogues are closed, and the children are taken on picnics. While picnicking the children play games and plant trees. What fun tree planting is!

Everybody helps. Some dig holes, some pour water, others help guide the sap-lings into the moist holes. When the trees are in place, everyone helps pack the rich soil around the tiny tree roots.

Israeli children know that trees are very important and serve many useful pur-poses. Some trees drain swamps to make Israel a healthier place in which to live. Others can be made into lumber with which to build new homes, schools, ships, etc. Other trees help to hold the soil in place so that the wind and flood cannot carry it away. Some trees bear fruit and give shade from the hot Israeli sun.

On Chamishah Asar B'Shevat, we too go on picnics and parties and enjoy the fruits of Israel.

We eat oranges, dates, figs and grapes, bokser (St. John's bread or carob pods), and cookies in the shapes of trees.

---

1. Today you probably know this as Tu B'Shevat, since Tu stands for 15.

STUFFED DATES

You won't need a stove to make this.

INGREDIENTS
dates
nuts
sugar

EQUIPMENT
knife
wax paper

HOW TO MAKE
1. Remove pits from the dates.
2. Put half a walnut or pecan in the cavity.
3. Close up the date.
4. Roll the dates in sugar; plain or powdered.

STUFFED PRUNES

INGREDIENTS

prunes
marshmallows
peanut butter
sugar

EQUIPMENT

double boiler
knife
wax paper

HOW TO MAKE

1. Steam some prunes in a double boiler for 10 minutes.
2. Cool them and remove the stones.
3. Stuff them with marshmallows or peanut butter.
4. Roll them in sugar on the wax paper.

PURIM

Many years ago, in the faraway land of Persia, there lived a king named Ahasuerus. One day the king decided that he needed a new queen, so he sent his messengers to look for the most beautiful maiden in the whole land of Persia.

They found a beautiful young Jewish girl named Esther, who was living with her uncle Mordecai. When the king saw lovely Esther, he fell in love with her immediately and chose her for his new queen.

At that time, the king's chief minister was a wicked man named Haman. He wanted everyone to bow down to him and almost everyone did. But Mordecai refused. Haman became very angry at Mordecai and at all the Jews. He decided to have all the Jews in the land of Persia killed. Lots were cast, and the thirteenth day of Adar was the chosen date for the terrible deed. Of course, the Jews were frightened; Mordecai begged Esther to save her people.

Soon the king noticed that the queen was unhappy. When he asked Esther what was worrying her, she replied' "O King, Haman is going to kill my people on the thirteenth day of Adar. He has built gallows on which to hang my Uncle Mordecai. Please save my people and my uncle." Ahasuerus did not want beautiful Esther to be unhappy. The king called his palace guards and ordered them to hang Haman on the very gallows he had prepared for Mordecai.

So on the thirteenth day of Adar, the Jews, instead of being killed, celebrated a happy holiday. They called the day "Purim," which means "lots."

Today, the holiday of Purim starts with the reading of the Megillah in the temple. Every time Haman's name is mentioned, the children stamp their feet, rattle their graggers, and make lots of noise.

After the reading of the Megillah, the fun really starts. In Israel, they stage outdoor carnivals and parades. In our homes, we celebrate by making a special Purim feast called a Seudah, and by sending Shalach Manos to our friends and relatives.

The traditional food for Purim is hamantaschen, a three-cornered cake filled with poppy or plum filling. Some say we eat hamantaschen because Haman wore a three-cornered hat; some even say that Haman's ears were three-cornered just like a donkey's ears.

HAMANTASCHEN

Follow the recipe for Chanukah cookies on page 41.

1. Roll the dough out thin.
2. Cut into rounds of 2½ inches.
3. Place a spoonful of hamantaschen filling in the center of each round.
4. Draw up three sides and pinch the sides together in the shape of a triangle.
5. Place on a buttered cookie sheet.
6. Bake at 375 degrees for 40 minutes.

HAMANTASCHEN PRUNE FILLING

INGREDIENTS

grated lemon rind
2 tablespoons lemon juice
½ pound prunes

EQUIPMENT

pot
colander
knife
cutting board
grater

HOW TO MAKE

1. Soak prunes in water for 12 hours.
2. Cook in water till soft.
3. Drain well.
4. Remove stones from prunes.
5. Dice the prunes.
6. Mix diced prunes with lemon rind and lemon juice.

PARTY LEMONADE

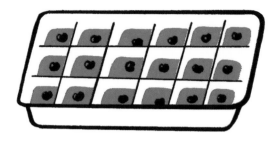

Are you making a Purim party? Serve this special lemonade and listen to the "oohs" and "ahs."

INGREDIENTS
frozen lemonade
maraschino cherries

EQUIPMENT
ice tray

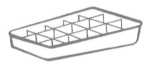

HOW TO MAKE
1. Place one cherry in each cube.
2. Fill ice tray with water.
3. Place in freezer.
4. Mix lemonade as per instructions on can.
5. Put a frozen cube in each glass of lemonade.

PURIM HAT COOKIES

The Jews in ancient Persia wore hats that looked something like these cookies.

INGREDIENTS

1 cup flour
shortening
marshmallows
½ cup quick oats
¼ cup butter
¼ cup brown sugar
¼ cup white sugar
½ tablespoon vanilla
1 egg
½ tablespoon salt

EQUIPMENT

big bowl
sifter
wooden spoon
paper towels
wax paper
cookie sheets
egg beater
measuring cup
measuring spoon

HOW TO MAKE

1. Preheat oven to 375 degrees.
2. Put ¼ cup butter in large bowl and beat till smooth.
3. Slowly add ¼ cup brown sugar and ¼ cup white sugar; beat till fluffy.
4. Beat in ½ tablespoon vanilla and ½ tablespoon salt.
5. Add egg and stir till completely mixed.
6. To mixture add ½ cup oats.
7. Sift flour onto wax paper.
8. Add 1 cup sifted flour to mixture and mix well.
9. Grease the cookie sheets.
10. Put spoonfuls of mixture on the cookie sheet; one spoonful to a cookie and flatten each one.
11. Bake for 8 minutes at 375 degrees.
12. Remove from stove, place a marshmallow on each cookie, and serve.

QUEEN ESTHER SALAD

INGREDIENTS

pineapple
almonds
cottage cheese
raisins

EQUIPMENT

knife
plate
can opener

HOW TO MAKE

1. Form a ball of cottage cheese and place in center of plate.
2. Place raisins in ball of cheese to make features of a face.
3. Cut a pineapple slice in half.
4. Crown the face with the half slice of pineapple.
5. Decorate Queen Esther's crown with almond halves.

NOAH'S ARK COOKIES

*Cookies are favorites of Shalach Manos baskets.
Make these animal cookies for your baskets.*

INGREDIENTS

1 package semi-sweet chocolate pieces
⅓ cup white corn syrup
2 ounces rice cereal

EQUIPMENT

double boiler
measuring cup
jelly roll pan
animal cutters

HOW TO MAKE

1. Melt chocolate in double boiler.
2. Stir in corn syrup.
3. Pour in rice cereal.
4. Mix until all kernels are coated.
5. Spread in jelly roll pan.
6. Cut with animal cutter.

PASSOVER

Passover is also known as the Festival of Freedom. On this holiday, at the Seder, we relive and retell the story of the Exodus.

We tell the story of the Israelites, who were slaves to the Pharaoh in the land of Egypt more than 3,000 years ago. Under the leadership of Moses, the Hebrews were at last set free.

They left in such great haste that they did not have time to leaven their bread.

When Moses and his followers reached the Red Sea, they received word that Pharaoh had changed his mind. He and his army were racing to recapture the Hebrews. Moses prayed to God. He then lifted his staff, and a miracle happened. The waters of the Red Sea parted, leaving a wide path through which Moses led his people to the other side. Behind them came the Egyptian army with its many chariots and horsemen. As Pharaoh's men were crossing the deep sea, Moses again lifted his staff. This time the water swiftly returned, and the entire Egyptian army was drowned.

Springtime is Passover time. Everyone is busy preparing for the festive holiday.

At last the long-awaited Seder night arrives. The table is set with a Passover plate with the five special Passover symbols: bitter herbs for the bitterness of slavery in the land of Egypt; a bone for the paschal lamb; charoset, which looks like the clay the Jews made into bricks; green herbs, which stand for the springtime; an egg, which is a symbol of life.

The leader of the Seder arranges three matzot in the beautiful embroidered matzoh cover and then sits down at the head of the table. All the people around the table open their Haggadahs. The Seder has begun.

The leader stands and, raising a wine cup, sings the Kiddush. Then the youngest child proudly asks the Four Questions and everyone reads the story of Passover.

During the meal, the Afikoman, which has been hidden by the Seder leader, disappears. It must be found before the Seder can be continued. Soon the leader opens the door to admit the Prophet Elijah, who visits each Jewish home on Seder night. At the end of the Seder everyone joins in singing the Passover songs.

Passover is the holiday most closely associated with food. During this holiday we omit all leaven from our meals. Dried beans, grains, bread, baking soda and yeast are forbidden. Instead of flour, we use matzoh products: matzoh meal, matzoh flour, matzoh cereal.

Passover is a busy time, with all the cooking and baking and cleaning. Mother and Father will appreciate all the help they can get.

Let's help by setting the Passover table. First we'll cover the table with a white tablecloth and set out the plates and silverware. Alongside each setting, place a wine cup and at the center of the table the special cup for Elijah the Prophet.

Now arrange the Seder plate with all the Passover symbols. Follow the picture and place each symbol in its correct position.

On the following page you will find the recipe for charoset.

Underneath the Seder plate place the matzoh cover with a matzoh in each of its three compartments. Don't forget to place a Haggadah at each setting so that everyone can participate in the Seder.

CHAROSET

INGREDIENTS

1 apple
½ cup finely chopped nuts
½ tablespoon cinnamon
1 tablespoon sugar
½ tablespoon wine
(or any kind of juice)

EQUIPMENT

grater
fork
paring knife
measuring cup
measuring spoon

HOW TO MAKE

1. Peel apple and grate.
2. Chop nuts very fine.
3. Mix the grated apple, chopped nuts, cinnamon, sugar and wine together.
4. Blend thoroughly until free of lumps.

MATZOH BREI

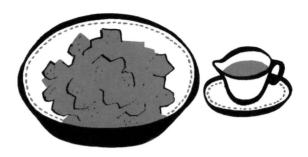

INGREDIENTS

2 matzot
boiling water
2 eggs
pepper
salt
honey
butter, shortening, oil, or fat

EQUIPMENT

colander
egg beater
large fry pan

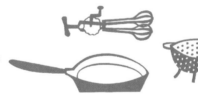

HOW TO MAKE

1. Break 2 matzot into medium-sized pieces and place in colander.
2. Pour hot water over them and drain quickly.
3. Beat eggs well.
4. Add beaten eggs to matzot.
5. Add salt and pepper to taste.
6. Heat a large fry pan and grease,
7. Add matzoh and egg mixture to hot fry pan.
8. Cook over low heat till brown on one side.
9. Turn gently and cook other side till brown.
10. Serve hot.
11. Pour honey over matzoh brei.

PASSOVER KUGEL

INGREDIENTS

3 matzot
1 egg yolk
1 egg white
1 apple
butter or shortening
salt
pepper

EQUIPMENT

large dish
beater
paring knife
chopping board
wax paper
casserole dish

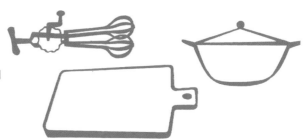

HOW TO MAKE

1. Soak matzot in water for 2 minutes.
2. Squeeze out as much water as possible.
3. Peel and dice the apple.
4. Add 1 tablespoon butter or shortening and the diced apple to the matzot.
5. Beat egg yolk into the mixture and season with salt and pepper.
6. Beat egg white until stiff.
7. Add the beaten egg white; handle egg white gently.
8. Pour into greased casserole dish.
9. Bake in slow oven for 1 hour or until top has a nice brown crust.

PASSOVER MACAROONS

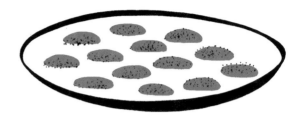

INGREDIENTS

four-ounce package shredded coconut
2 egg whites
½ cup powdered sugar
½ teaspoon lemon juice
butter, oil, or shortening

EQUIPMENT

glass bowl
measuring cup
cookie sheet
egg beater

HOW TO MAKE

1. Put egg whites into a bowl and beat till stiff.
2. Add sugar to stiff egg whites; blend.
3. Add the lemon and continue beating until light and smooth.
4. Add the shredded coconut; mix thoroughly.
5. Drop spoonfuls onto a greased cookie sheet.
6. Bake in an oven at 275 degrees for 40 minutes.

PEANUT BRITTLE

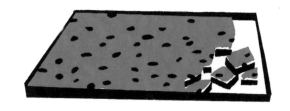

You can substitute any kind of nuts you wish.
Everybody likes a peanut brittle.
Make it for Passover.

INGREDIENTS

1 cup sugar
1 cup shelled peanuts
butter, oil, or shortening

EQUIPMENT

heavy iron frying pan
wooden spoon
oblong pan
measuring cup

HOW TO MAKE

1. Melt sugar in the frying pan over a low heat.
2. Stir the sugar with your wooden spoon as it melts.
3. When it is light brown, stir in the nuts.
4. Pour the mixture into a greased pan.
5. When it has cooled break the candy into pieces.

CANDIED APPLE WEDGES

Candied fruit slices are great favorites for Passover.
Try these apple wedges on your family.

INGREDIENTS

3 cups granulated sugar
1 ⅛ cups water
½ teaspoon salt
3 pared apples

EQUIPMENT

large saucepan
measuring cup
wire drain rack
wax paper
apple corer

HOW TO MAKE

1. In large saucepan place 2½ cups granulated sugar, salt and water.
2. Heat and stir till sugar dissolves.
3. Boil for ten minutes till you get a rich syrup.
4. Cut pared apple into eights lengthwise; trim and core.
5. Lay pieces into syrup and boil gently until most of syrup is absorbed.
6. Drain on rack in shallow pan.
7. Roll pieces in remaining half cup of sugar.
8. After apples dry for several hours, roll in sugar once more.

LAG B'OMER

L AG B'OMER is a gay, spring holiday. We celebrate it by picnicking, going on hikes, and playing with bows and arrows. The holiday commemorates the day the plague among Rabbi Akiva's students stopped.

Akiva was a fearless rabbi who lived in a sad and troubled period of Jewish history. The Romans had conquered the land of Israel, captured Jerusalem, and destroyed the temple. Many Jews were killed and the study of Torah was forbidden.

Akiva hid in the forest and continued to study and teach the Torah. His students disguised themselves as hunters by carrying bows and arrows. Should the Roman soldiers find them, this was their excuse for being in the forest.

One time a plague struck Rabbi Akiva's students and killed many of them. Suddenly on Lag B'Omer the plague stopped and the study of Torah was continued again.

Lag B'Omer means "the thirty-third day of counting the Omer." This holiday is also known as the Scholars' Holiday in honor of Rabbi Akiva and his fearless students.

One the most famous of Rabbi Akiva's students was Bar Kochba. He was a very brave, fearless, and strong warrior. Under his leadership the Jews fought the Romans for more than three years. Bar Kochba and his men recaptured Jerusalem and started to rebuild the Temple that the Romans had destroyed.

But the Romans returned with more and more soldiers. The Jews retreated to the fortress city of Betar. On the ninth day of Av (Tisha B'Av), the Romans captured the city and killed Bar Kochba.

There are no traditional foods for Lag B'Omer. Instead we pack picnic lunches and eat out of doors just as Rabbi Akiva and his students did thousands of years ago.

Lag B'Omer is the time we all go on picnics. Picnics mean sandwiches. Here are a few hints on sandwich making which can make your picnic lunch a success.

HINTS FOR SANDWICH MAKING

1. Make your sandwiches from a variety of breads and rolls.
2. Cream butter before spreading.
3. Avoid making sandwiches with moist fillings in advance, since the bread becomes soggy.
4. Wrap each sandwich in wax paper.
5. Use a variety of fillings.
6. Vegetables such as tomatoes, lettuce and cucumbers should be prepared and added just before serving.

SANDWICH FILLINGS

1. Cream cheese and lox.
2. Cream cheese and jelly.
3. Sliced egg and tomato.
4. Egg and diced celery.
5. Tuna, celery and mayonnaise.
6. Sardines and eggs.
7. Chopped salmon and onions.
8. Peanut butter and jelly.
9. Swiss cheese and mustard.

LAG B'OMER
BULL'S EYE

*Rabbi Akiva's scholars used to disguise themselves
as hunters. With their bows and arrows,
they used to shoot at targets such as this bull's eye.
Try this recipe. I'll bet it hits the target.*

INGREDIENTS
white bread
butter
egg
salt

EQUIPMENT
fry pan
small glass

HOW TO MAKE
1. Use a glass and cut a hole in a slice of white bread.
2. Grease the fry pan with butter.
3. Place bread with hole in pan and toast till bottom side is brown.
4. Turn bread over, brown side up.
5. Crack the egg and drop the egg into the hole.
6. Fry until egg is done.

CHOCOLATE PEPPERMINTS

Try these peppermints on your Lag B'Omer picnic.

INGREDIENTS

4 squares bitter chocolate
⅛ cup condensed milk
⅛ cup honey
⅛ teaspoon salt
few drops peppermint extract

EQUIPMENT

double boiler
wooden mixing spoon
measuring cup
measuring spoon
wax paper

HOW TO MAKE

1. Melt chocolate in a double boiler.
2. Stir in condensed milk, honey, salt, and peppermint.
3. Allow to cool and drop chocolate from a teaspoon on wax paper.
4. Make about two dozen chocolate pieces.

SHAVUOT

Shavuot (Festival of Weeks) is celebrated seven weeks after the Passover holiday. It marks the birthday of the Ten Commandments, which Moses received on Mount Sinai. At that time, Moses, at God's command, gathered the Israelites at the foot of the mountain. They waited and waited. On the third day, a thick cloud settled on the mountain. The earth shook. Everyone trembled. Amid thunder and lightning, they heard the voice of God calling out the Ten Commandments.

Shavuot also celebrates the Harvest Festival; in this season, the Jewish farmers journeyed to the Temple with the first fruits of their fields. These gifts were collected by the priests and were distributed to the poor people of the land. Shavuot is also known as Chag Habikurim, which means "first ripe fruits."

Today, we celebrate Shavuot by attending synagogue, where we read the Ten Commandments and a special hymn called Akdamut. This prayer describes the wisdom of the Torah and the coming of the Messiah.

It is also customary to read the Book of Ruth, which describes the harvest in ancient Israel and tells how the poor people of the land were allowed to pick up the fallen ears of grain during the harvest.

To remind us of the Harvest Festival, homes and synagogues are decorated with green leaves, flowers and fruits.

Religious schools hold their confirmation and graduation exercises during this season.

Because the Torah has been compared to "milk and honey," sweet dairy dishes are usually served on Shavuot. Blintzes (cheese-filled pancakes) are a favorite dish.

CRACKER CHEESE BLINTZES

INGREDIENTS

10 soda crackers
4 eggs
salt
½ pound dry cottage cheese (or Ricotta or Farmer's cheese)
2 tablespoons butter
cinnamon
butter, oil, or shortening

EQUIPMENT

2 mixing bowls
grater
griddle

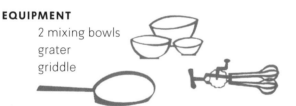

HOW TO MAKE

1. Beat 2 eggs well.
2. Add ¼ cup milk and a pinch of salt to the beaten egg.

TO MAKE FILLING

1. Combine cottage cheese, 2 eggs, 2 tablespoons sugar, and pinch of cinnamon.
2. Mix well.
3. Place a quantity of filling between 2 crackers.
4. Dip cracker and cheese sandwich in egg and milk mixture.
5. Place sandwich on hot greased griddle.
6. Fry on both sides till brown.

TOMATO FLOWER SALAD

Shavuot is a time for serving "harvest fruit."
Vegetables, fruits, and dairy dishes are traditional delights.

INGREDIENTS
tomatoes
paprika
cottage cheese
French dressing
lettuce

EQUIPMENT
knife

HOW TO MAKE
1. Cut away core of tomato.
2. Cut the tomato into wedges. Do not cut the wedges all the way through.
3. Place wedged tomato on washed lettuce leaf.
4. Fill tomato with cottage cheese.
5. Sprinkle with paprika and French dressing.

QUICK TRUFFLES

*The Torah is said to be
"nutritious as honey, and as good as milk."
Try these "nutritious" truffles with a glass of milk.*

INGREDIENTS

1 package semi-sweet chocolate bits
⅜ cup sweetened condensed milk
½ cup chopped walnuts
½ teaspoon vanilla extract
few grains of salt

EQUIPMENT

double boiler
measuring cup
measuring spoon
wax paper
shallow pan
wooden spoon

HOW TO MAKE

1. Melt chocolate in double boiler.
2. Stir in condensed milk, walnuts, vanilla, and salt.
3. Pour into wax lined pan.
4. Cool for a few hours.
5. When firm, cut into squares.

APPENDIX:

MODERN JEWISH RECIPES

ROSH HASHANA

Not only is dipping apples in honey a traditional way to celebrate Rosh Hashana, it's also a great opportunity to pay attention to—and really taste—both the apples and honey. Some apples are tangy, or sweet, or fragrant, or crunchy, red, green, or even golden. The honey can be mild or strong, light-colored or dark, with its flavor and aroma depending on what the bees were feeding on when they made it. Lemon juice will keep the apples from turning brown; and even though the apple is sour, the honey you dip into is lovely and sweet.

LET'S DIP APPLES IN HONEY!
Serves 4-6 people

INGREDIENTS
> 2–3 medium-sized apples with their skins on
> ¼–½ lemon
> a few spoonfuls of honey

EQUIPMENT
> cutting board
> paring knife
> lemon juicer
> small bowl
> plate

HOW TO MAKE
1. Cut the apples into wedges with their skins left on; using a paring knife cut the insides/seeds out; squeeze the lemon over the apples and toss well.
2. Arrange the apple slices on a plate.
3. Put the honey in a small bowl or saucer.
4. When it's time to serve, have everyone dip their apple wedge into the honey, and then eat it up.

During Sukkot, we take delight in eating the fruit and vegetables of the season, even more so if we're able to eat outside, in the Sukkah.

BAKED SWEET POTATOES
Serves 4 people

INGREDIENTS
4 small- to medium-sized sweet potatoes,
½–1 teaspoon vegetable oil for rubbing
a few shakes of soy sauce and a sprinkling of toasted sesame seeds
    to taste, or a pat or two of butter, as desired

EQUIPMENT
baking pan
fork
paring knife

HOW TO MAKE
1. Wash the sweet potatoes, dry them, and then, using a fork, poke them in several places all over.
2. Rub the potatoes with the oil and place in a baking pan just big enough to hold all of the sweet potatoes.
3. Heat the oven to 400F/200C.
4. Place the sweet potatoes in the oven and bake until they are tender, which will depend on the size and shape of the sweet potato. This should be about 40-60 minutes or until they feel soft when you press them with the fork (remember that the potato juices will leak out and form little burnt patches in the pan; not to worry, just scrape them off when you wash the pan).
5. To serve the sweet potatoes, slash them on top with the knife, and dress with a splash of soy sauce and a sprinkling of sesame seeds, or with a pat of butter for melting.

RAW VEGETABLES AND HUMMUS:
DIP AND CRUNCH!

Serves 6-8 people

Dipping raw vegetables is fun, and also a good way to taste lots of different ones. There are so many vegetables to choose from and dips as well. For example, you might like guacamole (made from avocado), spinach ranch-dip, or a mild salsa, and maybe hummus? Is there a better way to eat hummus than dipping crunchy vegetables into it?

Choose an assortment of raw vegetables; the bonus is that if you have extra vegetables after everyone has dipped and eaten, the next day you can always make a nice vegetable soup or salad with them. Here's a suggestion for preparing a beautiful plate of vegetables with hummus!

INGREDIENTS

carrot sticks or 1-2 medium-large carrots, peeled and cut into sticks
1 regular cucumber, peeled and sliced into spears, or a box of baby
    cucumbers, which are probably small enough to eat whole
1 red bell pepper, seeds and stem removed and discarded, cut into strips
a handful of sugar snap peas: so crunchy and sweet
1 stalk of celery, cut in half lengthwise, then up and down into sticks
8-10 baby Romaine lettuce spears, or as desired
one 8 oz / 250 g or 250 ml container of your favorite hummus
one small container of Greek yogurt

EQUIPMENT

serving platter
bowl
fork

HOW TO MAKE

1. Arrange the vegetables on a serving platter.
2. Pour/spoon the hummus into a bowl, and with a fork or a spoon, beat it up until it gets a little bit fluffy.
3. Next, add the Greek yogurt and mix it well. This is the secret to a delicious hummus!
4. Spoon the hummus in a serving bowl and serve it with the vegetable platter.

SUKKOT FRUIT BOWL

When you are decorating the Sukkah with the fruits of the season such as pomegranate, persimmons (either the crisp fuyu or the soft hachiya), apples, and pears, be sure to save some to eat in the Sukkah.

—

CHANUKAH

CRANBERRY APPLESAUCE
Serves 4-6 people

To go with the fried latkes of Chanukah, cranberry applesauce is a unique version of traditional; strawberry applesauce is, too. Either one is delish!

INGREDIENTS
½–1 cup / 250 g or 250 ml fresh or frozen cranberries
about 2 cups / 500 ml applesauce (homemade or store-bought, sweetened or unsweetened, as you like)
2 tablespoons sugar or honey (or to taste, if the applesauce is not sweetened)

EQUIPMENT
saucepan

HOW TO MAKE
1. Place the cranberries in a saucepan with the honey or sugar. Cover and cook together over medium low heat until the berries are hot and some start to pop. If they seem like they are burning, add a spoonful or two of water or orange juice.
2. Remove from heat, let cool, and then mix with the applesauce. Chill till ready to serve.

VARIATION: STRAWBERRY APPLESAUCE DIP FOR LATKES
Instead of cranberries, use frozen strawberries, defrosted instead of cooked. Combine the defrosted strawberries with the applesauce, sugar to taste, and chill until ready to serve.

FROZEN WHITE—OR DARK—CHOCOLATE BARK WITH DRIED FRUIT
Serves 4-6 people

White chocolate is prettier, but dark is irresistible, and who doesn't love milk chocolate? The choice, with these delicacies, is yours. And here's an interesting thought: chocolate comes from pods that grow on special trees, so eating it is really celebrating the holiday of the trees!

INGREDIENTS
    12 oz / 375 g good quality white (or dark, or milk) chocolate
    1 cup / 250 g chopped mixed dried fruit of choice (for example: dried
        figs, raisins, cranberries, apricots, kiwi, pineapple, goji berries, mango)

EQUIPMENT
    cookie or baking sheet
    parchment paper
    microwave-safe bowl
    wooden spoon for stirring

HOW TO MAKE
1. Line a cookie or baking sheet with parchment paper. Set aside.
2. Break up the chocolate and put the pieces in a microwave-safe bowl.
3. Put the microwave on High/Cook for 45 seconds.
4. Take the bowl out, stir it up, and then put it back in for another 45 seconds.
5. Take it out again and stir it; the chocolate should have melted completely, but if it hasn't, microwave it one more time. (Alternatively, you can melt the chocolate in a double boiler over simmering water on the stovetop, but microwaving is fool-proof, while on the stovetop the chocolate can get grainy or clump up.)
6. Pour the melted chocolate onto the paper and sprinkle the fruit and nuts over it.
7. Put pan in the freezer until the chocolate hardens.
8. Crack the bark into pieces and keep it in the freezer, in an airtight container, until ready to eat.

PURIM

SHALACH MANOS (MISHLOACH MANOT)

Shalach Manos (in Israel Mishloach Manot) is the giving of plates of food/treats for the holiday. Usually it is sweets, a selection of homemade and purchased simple cookies and confections, wrapped up on the plate appealingly, like a present. The favorite types of sweets are traditional Jewish treats, which are treats from whatever your own Jewish heritage offers. Hamantaschen, of course, and Mandelbrot, chocolate chip cookies, whatever your favorites!

Giving special foods is a way to strengthen the bond with other Jews, and it is a unifying force since we all love to give, and we all love to get, and we are all doing just that!

SEEDED CRISP-CHEESE MORSELS

Serves 4-6 people

Queen Esther ate seeds in order to keep kosher in the palace (and dried fruit, as there was little fresh fruit in season at the time, and to keep kosher she ate only raw foods). So, eating seeds and dried fruit is a tradition for Purim.
This is a delicious seed and cheese treat—a crisp cracker-like morsel made only of cheese and seeds.

INGREDIENTS

    12 oz / 375 g hard cheese, such as Jack or Cheddar,
        or any medium- to hard cheese you like
    approximately 3 oz / 90 g grated Parmesan, Asiago or Pecorino
        Romano cheese
    ½ cup / 125 g or more, if and as desired, mixed seeds: sesame,
        sunflower, pumpkin, cumin, you name it!

EQUIPMENT

    shredder or cheese grater
    nonstick baking sheet or silpat
    cooling plate or rack

HOW TO MAKE

    1. Shred the Jack or Cheddar cheese.

2. Arrange the cheese and seeds in little mounds in a single layer on a large nonstick baking sheet, or on a silpat (you don't want it to stick). The cheeses will probably run into each other as they melt, but it doesn't matter: you want it to be crisp, and the more uneven it is, the crisper the edges will be.
3. Turn on the oven to 400F/200C, and bake until the cheese melts and gets crisp, about 10 minutes depending on your oven. Check every few minutes so that it browns but does not burn.
4. Remove from the oven, and then, using a spatula, remove the melted cheese and seed crisps to a plate or a rack to cool. Don't worry if they break up; they will not look pretty, but they will taste delicious.
5. Store in an airtight container and eat whenever you're tempted.

—

PASSOVER

ASHKENAZI CHAROSET, WITH TRAIL MIX
Serves 6-8 people

INGREDIENTS
3 apples, cored but unpeeled, diced
1-2 sticks/ribs celery, finely diced
about 1½ cups / 350 g dried fruit/nut/seed mix or any very delicious trail mix (with dried fruit, but without bits of chocolate, other candies, and of course no hametz in it)
5-6 tablespoons sweet red wine for Passover (or any dry red wine or red grape juice or other fruit juice)
1½ teaspoon ground cinnamon
1-2 tablespoons sugar/honey, or to taste

EQUIPMENT
mixing bowl

HOW TO MAKE
1. Combine the ingredients, mix well, and chill till ready to use.

MATZO WITH CREAM CHEESE, STRAWBERRY PRESERVES, AND FRESH STRAWBERRIES

Serves 1-2 people

Matzo spread with cream cheese and jam is so good; add a topping of fresh strawberries and it becomes special.

INGREDIENTS
   1 piece of matzo
   cream cheese, enough for a thickish layer on the matzo
   2 tablespoons, or to taste, strawberry preserves
   about 10 fresh strawberries, depending on their size, hulled and sliced

EQUIPMENT
   spreading knife
   plate

HOW TO MAKE
   1. Break the matzo into two pieces.
   2. Spread it with cream cheese, then with strawberry preserves.
   3. Top with the sliced strawberries and eat right away.

—

LAG B'OMER

The holiday of springtime, of being out and about, hiking, walking, enjoying the warm days. And when you are hiking, you bring a sandwich, or two, or as many as you have hiking buddies.

SANDWICHES

Each sandwich serves 1, or if shared, serves 2
(along with other sandwiches or dishes).

CUCUMBER AND GARLIC-CREAM CHEESE OR GOAT CHEESE

INGREDIENTS
>2 slices of good, fresh French bread (baguette)
>1-2 tablespoons of garlicky soft cheese such as Alouette, Boursin, or a soft herbed goat cheese (I like lots of the garlicky cheese spread; you might, too)
>about ¼ cucumber, cut into thin slices

EQUIPMENT
>spreading knife
>plate

HOW TO MAKE
1. Spread the soft cheese generously over both slices of bread.
2. Top one slice with a layer of cucumbers, then close the sandwich up with the second cheese-spread bread.
3. Wrap in waxed or parchment paper, and pack for later.

CALIFORNIA SANDWICH:
AVOCADO, SUNFLOWER SEEDS, AND CHEESE

INGREDIENTS

2 slices grainy whole-grain (and seeded if you like) bread

1-2 tablespoons mayonnaise, for spreading

1 ripe tomato, sliced

about 2 oz / 60 g cheese, sliced: choose Jack, Swiss, Cheddar, Gouda, whichever you like

½ ripe avocado, seed removed, spooned out of shell

1 tablespoon toasted hulled sunflower seeds

EQUIPMENT

spreading knife

plate

waxed or parchment paper

HOW TO MAKE

1. Lay the two slices of bread on a plate and lightly spread with mayonnaise.
2. On one, place sliced tomato, then cheese, avocado, and a sprinkling of sunflower seeds.
3. Top with the other piece of mayonnaise-spread bread and pat gently but firmly to hold it together
4. Wrap in waxed or parchment paper.

WHOLE-WHEAT PITA WITH PEANUT BUTTER (OR ALMOND, OR CASHEW BUTTER) AND BANANA

Sometimes I like to add shredded carrot and a drizzle of honey to this as well.

INGREDIENTS
1 whole-wheat pita or 2 slices whole-grain bread
several tablespoons peanut, almond, or cashew butter, or as desired
1 banana

EQUIPMENT
knife for cutting bread
spreading knife
plate
waxed or parchment paper

HOW TO MAKE
1. Cut a slice into the pita so that you have a pocket, or lay out the two slices of whole-grain bread.
2. Spread the nut butter generously in the pita or on the bread slices.
3. Peel and slice the banana; then add the banana slices to the nut butter filling either in the pita or on top of the bread.
4. Close up and wrap in waxed or parchment paper.

—

SHAVUOT

We celebrate Shavuot with treats made from dairy, milk, and cheese.

SWEET PITA CRISPS DELIGHT
Serves 2-4 people

INGREDIENTS
2 oz / 60 g, approximately, good-quality dark chocolate
2 whole-wheat pitas
a teaspoon or two of extra-virgin olive oil
1 ½-2 tablespoons sugar (vanilla sugar if you have it)
8 oz / 250 g whole-milk ricotta cheese
12-15 dried apricots, cut into thin strips or chopped

EQUIPMENT
grater
cutting knife
plate
baking sheet
waxed or parchment paper

HOW TO MAKE
1. Grate the chocolate on the large holes of a grater; set aside.
2. Slit the pitas carefully around their edges to make two thin pieces of bread.
3. Drizzle a bit of olive oil on the cut side and press the cut sides together to make the small amount of oil go further and to keep it from getting greasy
4. Arrange the pita halves on a baking sheet, oiled side up; cut and sprinkle with sugar.
5. Broil until the sugar melts; do not let it brown too much or it will burn.
6. Remove from broiler—do not eat right away, or even touch the hot sugar, it will burn you! That is how hot melted sugar gets!
7. Spoon the ricotta on top, spreading it down evenly
8. Sprinkle with the apricot strips first and then the chocolate.
9. Eat right away.

LOCHSHON AND CHEESE, THEN AND NOW: NOODLES WITH COTTAGE CHEESE

When I was a child, my favorite dish in the whole wide world was buttered butterfly noodles (also known as bowties), tossed with cottage cheese. Then I grew up and started to make changes to this recipe. One day I thought: "I'm going to try soba noodles, those Japanese buckwheat noodles." It turned out GREAT. Another day it was peas: "I wonder what peas will taste like in this?" (Also great, it turned out!) So my own family grew up eating buckwheat soba, cottage cheese, and peas. Both ways are wonderful; try them both, and see which one turns out to be your favorite!

BOWTIES AND COTTAGE CHEESE

Serves 4 people

INGREDIENTS
12 oz / 350 g bowtie pasta
butter to taste, as desired
12 oz / 350 g container cottage cheese, or as desired

EQUIPMENT
pot for boiling pasta
bowl

HOW TO MAKE
1. Boil the pasta till just cooked through but not soft (have a grownup help you with this). The Italians call this stage *al dente* (meaning you can feel the pasta still with your teeth!).
2. Drain the pasta.
3. Place in a bowl or return to the pan and toss with butter to melt.
4. Add the cottage cheese and mix well, then serve (I like salt and pepper with mine, but you may or may not).

BUCKWHEAT SOBA WITH COTTAGE CHEESE AND PEAS

Serves 4 people

INGREDIENTS
12 oz / 350 g buckwheat soba
butter to taste, as desired (or olive oil)
½ cup / 250 g (or more) frozen peas, as you like
12 oz / 350 g cottage cheese or as desired

EQUIPMENT
pot for boiling pasta
bowl

HOW TO MAKE
1. Boil the buckwheat soba till it is just tender, and then drain as above.
2. Toss with the butter or olive oil, and the peas (you want the heat of the soba to defrost the peas).
3. Add the cottage cheese and serve (again: you may like salt and pepper, you may not; add it according to taste).

WHITE BREAD BLINTZES

Serves 4-6 people

Here's a really easy blintzes recipe you can make in just a few minutes!

INGREDIENTS

    1 container of soft cream cheese
    1 tablespoon of milk
    ½ a loaf of sliced white bread
    1 teaspoon cinnamon
    2 tablespoons sugar (regular or brown)
    ½ cup of butter, melted
    ½ teaspoon vanilla extract
    nonstick cooking spray

EQUIPMENT

    baking tray
    2 bowls
    cutting board
    bread knife

HOW TO MAKE

1. Preheat the oven to 350F/175C.
2. Spray the baking tray with nonstick cooking spray.
3. Cut the crusts off the bread, and then flatten each slice.
4. In one bowl, mix the soft cream cheese with the milk and vanilla extract.
5. In another bowl, mix the sugar and cinnamon.
6. Spread the cream cheese mix onto each flattened slice of bread.
7. Roll each slice, dip it in the melted butter for just a second and then dip in the sugar and cinnamon mix.
8. Place the rolled slices on the baking tray.
9. Bake for 10 minutes.

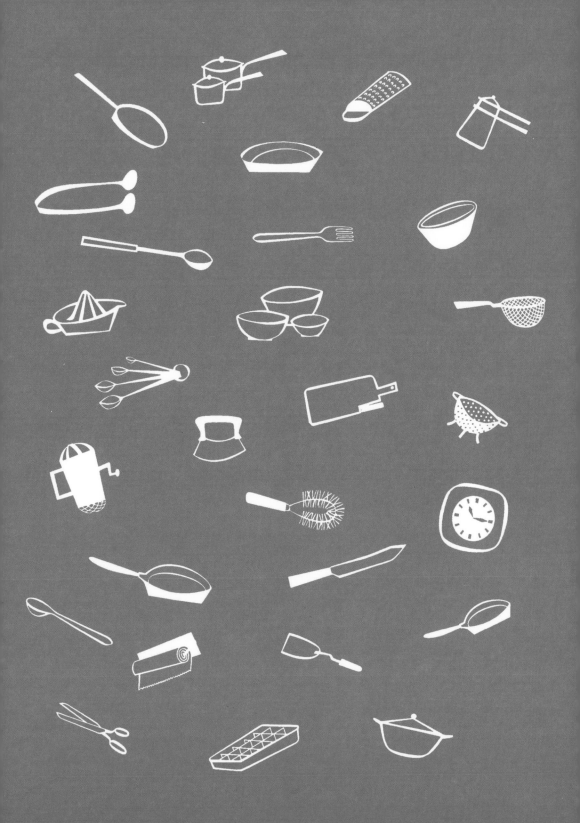